Last Chance

to Fly

RARE AND HISTORIC AIRLINERS STILL IN USE

Robert Mitchell

DestinWorld
publishing

First Edition 2017
ISBN 978-0-9955307-7-5

British Library Cataloguing-in-Publication Data
A catalogue record for this book is available from the British Library.

Published by Destinworld Publishing Ltd.
www.destinworld.com

Research by Robert Mitchell
Cover design by John Wright
All photographs © Matthew Falcus unless otherwise stated
Interior design: Cover&Layout, **www.coverandlayout.com**
Printed and bound in Great Britain by Marston Book Services Ltd, Oxfordshire

Last Chance
to Fly

Contents

Introduction

Welcome to the second edition of *Last Chance to Fly* – the enthusiast's guide to finding and flying on rare and historic airliners around the world.

Experiencing flight on an older aircraft can be a memorable experience, particularly on aircraft which are truly historic. Even flying an aircraft type which was prevalent in our younger days but is now a rare sight can bring back great memories of the sounds and smells of a previous generation of airliner.

Groups of people now gather online and on specially arranged tours in order to experience flying on older aircraft before it's too late. We therefore hope that this book will provide some useful background to the possibilities which still exist, albeit decreasing by the year, to fly on a special airliner.

The Scope of Aircraft Listed

Since the first edition of this book appeared in 2011 many classic airliners have ceased flying passengers altogether. Particularly types such as the Boeing 707 and McDonnell Douglas MD-11. However, we have also added new types to this edition which have become 'historic' or rare over recent years. Some types may be considered relatively new to the reader, however their scarcity leads us to believe they deserve a place in this book to offer a last chance to fly before it's gone completely!

As always, our research has been thorough. Yet we accept there may be errors, and since change occurs so rapidly in the airline industry we cannot be held responsible for aircraft types being retired by airlines following the book's publication.

Updates

Please forward any updates, corrections and missing details for future editions to: **info@destinworld.com**

Airbus A300

First flying in 1972, the A300 was the first product of the new Airbus consortium in Europe, and one of a new range of widebody airliners emerging. The B1 was the initial design, but after only two examples the B2 became the initial standard. Quickly becoming the standard production model of the Airbus A300, the B4 was first flown in 1974.

Later models include the A300B4-600 which had newer engines and increased seating capacity through using part of the A310 fuselage.

Asia & Middle East

The best place to fly on an Airbus A300 now is in Iran.

Iran Air still operates A300B4-200 and B4-605R models awaiting replacement by more modern types.

Mahan Air still operate the Airbus A300B4-603 on routes internally within Iran and on flights to Dubai, UAE.

Meraj Air operates two A300B4-622R examples, EP-SIF and EP-SIG, on the Tehran, IKA to Istanbul route.

Qeshm Air operate five A300B4-605R examples in a very smart colour scheme. These Iranian Airbus A300s have been operating on other international services to Europe, but for how much longer?

Airbus A310

Technically a variant of the A300 (the A300B10), the A310 features a shorter fuselage and tail fin, and a new wing design. It was offered initially in the -200 variant, with the -300 becoming standard later.

Production of the A310 ran from 1983 to 1998, during which time 255 aircraft were built. Most today fly for FedEx Express as freighters, however some examples still carry passengers.

Asia & Middle East

Iran Air continues to operate EP-IBL on some domestic and European schedules.

Taban Air of Iran operate a sole example, EP-TBH, on flights from Tehran to Europe

Yemenia is not an airline many will want to travel on, but nevertheless operates a single A310.

Europe

SATA Air Azores operates three examples in use on scheduled domestic routes within Portugal and the Azores, and on transatlantic flights to Boston, USA and Toronto, Canada. The fleet has recently been put up for sale, with all due to be removed by May 2018.

USA & Canada

Air Transat operate a fleet of Airbus A310-300s on various transatlantic and Caribbean routes, including regular flights to the UK and Europe.

Airbus A318

Only 3 airlines now fly the Airbus A318 – the smallest member of the A320 family of aircraft. Originally envisaged as a competitor to regional jets for airlines with crews already trained on the A319/20, sales were not forthcoming at a large scale. For the time being it's relatively easy to fly on the 'baby bus'.

Europe

Air France has been the largest operator of the type. It is seen on scheduled services out of Paris to airports around Europe.

British Airways has reduced its fleet to a single example which flies the flagship BA1/2 flights between London City and New York JFK, with a technical stop in Shannon. It is in a First Class layout.

TAROM operates 4 examples from Bucharest, including on the route to London Heathrow.

Titan Airways recently took delivery of one of the former British Airways A318s and will fly it on charter services, mostly in a VIP layout.

Airbus A340

Developed alongside the Airbus A330, the A340 was part of the manufacturer's bid to steal a chunk of the long-haul market from Boeing at a time when airlines were retiring older Lockheed L1011s and McDonnell Douglas DC-10s from service.

It was believed four engines would be more popular with passengers on long overseas flights, however changes in Extended Twin Operations (ETOPS) rules allowing twin aircraft to fly further meant the A330 (and its rivals) were always more popular than the A340, which was more expensive to operate.

Models of A340 included the original -200, closely followed by the -300. Both were considered quite underpowered.

Later, the long-range, higher capacity -500 and -600 variants entered the scene, offering a slight renaissance for the type. However, many airlines have now replaced their aircraft with newer generation twins.

Airbus A340-200

Africa

Air Leisure, an Egyptian leisure airline, is now the only passenger operator of the A340-200. They have two examples of the type based at Cairo which fly to various destinations in the Far East. It is normally only possible to book flights with them as part of a package deal.

The airline will soon focus on A330s for widebody operations.

Airbus A340-300

Africa

Air Madagascar operates two leased A340-300s on its principal long-haul services. They are expected to be replaced by the end of 2018.

Air Mauritius flies three examples, which will imminently be replaced by A350-900s.

South African Airways has eight -300s flying alongside its -600s on routes from Johannesburg and Cape Town.

Asia & Middle East

Kuwait Airways still operate two examples

Mahan Air's A340-300s work alongside its -600s on routes to Europe and the Far East from Tehran.

Philippine Airlines for the time being fly their -300s to Europe and North America, but will be replaced in 2018.

Syrianair. Former Mahan Air and Olympic Airlines aircraft were recently sourced, allowing the airline to operate flights to Dubai and other destinations. It is not recommended to try and fly them, however.

Central & South America
Aerolineas Argentinas has a small fleet of A340-300s in service which will be retired in 2018.

Surinam Airways relies on a single A340-300, PZ-TCR, for its long-haul link to Amsterdam Schiphol.

Europe
Air France was the largest operator of the type, but has been actively reducing its fleet over recent years. Nine examples were still flying to the Americas out of Paris at the time of writing.

Air Plus Ultra is a Spanish airline with a fleet of two A340-300s flying services out of Barcelona to Cuba, Chile and Peru.

Edelweiss Air are flying their former Swiss International A340-300s on North American, Mexican and Asian routes.

Lufthansa operates their -300s on various flights to the USA and Asia, with some flying under the 'Cityline' offshoot.

SAS Scandinavian Airlines uses eight A340-300s on long-haul services from its main bases as Copenhagen, Oslo and Stockholm. Recently refurbished, they are likely to remain flying into the 2020s.

Swiss International Airlines will now carry on operating five examples longer than anticipated, with refurbished cabin interiors.

Some examples were sold to Edelweiss Air recently.

TAP Portugal's four examples fly almost exclusively on the airline's flights from Lisbon to Sao Paulo and Luanda.

THY Turkish Airlines has reduced its fleet of A340-300s to two aircraft, with retirement anticipated.

Oceania & Pacific
Air Tahiti Nui has three examples flying long-haul services to Paris and Los Angeles, although their fleet will be retired soon.

Airbus A340-500
Asia & Middle East
AZAL Azerbaijan Airlines flies two of the best looking A340s out of Baku. They can often be seen flying to Europe.

Etihad Airways uses two examples, A6-EHC and A6-EHD, although for how much longer?

Airbus A340-600
Africa
South African Airways sees the type as their flagship long-haul aircraft. As well as routes to Europe, Australia and the Americas, it is also sometimes possible to fly it on the Johannesburg-Cape Town route.

Asia & Middle East
Mahan Air in Iran obtained a number of second-hand examples for flights across Europe and Asia.

Etihad Airways is reducing its fleet of A340s, but you can still find them operating from Abu Dhabi to a number of destinations.

Qatar Airways operate four examples out of Doha.

Europe
Iberia flies its A340-600s from Madrid to destinations in North and South America, the Far East, and also a daily flight to London Heathrow.

Lufthansa's A340-600 fleet is slowly being retired. It is based at Munich for flights to the Americas and Asia.

Virgin Atlantic Airways are also retiring their A340s in favour of Boeing 787s. For the time being the remaining fleet flies out of London Heathrow.

Antonov An-12

Mostly seen as a cargo aircraft, the large, four-engine turboprop An-12 has been made available for special enthusiast charters recently. As such, we include it here as a rare aircraft to fly.

Over 1,200 were built, yet very few are still seen in active service today.

Europe

Ruby Star is an airline based at Minsk, Belarus. Its An-12 aircraft are sometimes chartered by enthusiast tours, such as those offered by Merlintours.

Antonov An-24/26

This popular twin-turboprop airliner of 1950s design saw service across Eastern Europe, the Soviet states and Asia through its lifetime. Of the 1,300 built very few remain in passenger service. The same goes for its An-26 and An-30 stablemates, which mostly operate as cargo and military transports.

Asia & Middle East

Air Koryo flies the type. Flights on the airline are only accessible through an organised tour, such as those offered by Juche Travel Services.

Scat Airlines of Kazakhstan are flying three An-24RVs out of Almaty.

Europe

Genex is an An-26 operator based at Minsk, Belarus. Aviation charters have been known to use its aircraft on occasion.

Motor Sich Airlines of Ukraine operate An-24RVs out of Kiev Zhulany airport on various routes, such as Kiev-Zaprozhia. One of the aircraft has recently been refurbished, hinting it will be flying for a while still.

Antonov An-72/74

© Dmitriy Pichugin

Intended as a replacement for the An-26, the -72 is a regional jet airliner from the 1970s which did not see much success. Its unusual engine layout, placed on top of the high wings, makes it a distinctive airliner to fly on.

The An-74 was the military transport variant of this aircraft family. Again, few were built.

Asia & Middle East

Pouya Air in Iran flies the An-74. It is not easy to ascertain the routes or schedules of the aircraft, or how to book a flight on it. Organised aviation tours of Iran may be the only option.

Europe

Motor Sich Airlines in Ukraine operate a single An-72 example. Again, it seems difficult to plan an organise a flight on the aircraft, however the Kiev-Zaprozhia route is often served by it.

Antonov An-140

© Dmitry A. Mottl

Developed in the 1990s as Antonov's answer to the regional turboprop market so popular in the West, the An-140 is a twin airliner capable of carrying around 50 passengers, or an equivalent amount of cargo. It was designed for unprepared airstrips. Only 34 were built.

Europe

Motor Sich Airlines is the sole operator of the type in the world. Although flying on a Motor Sich Airlines An-140 (or any of their aircraft, for that matter) seems very tricky to arrange and plan.

Antonov An-148/158

© Oleg V. Belyakov – AirTeamImages

First flying in 2004, the Antonov An-148 is a twin-jet regional airliner capable of flying up to 2,400 miles with 68-85 passengers. It featured a modern fly-by-wire system and two-man cockpit, yet could easily handle unprepared airstrips. Just over 40 examples were built.

A stretched variant, the An-158, emerged in 2010 and was capable of carrying 99 passengers. It also featured wingtip fences and other improvements.

Asia & Middle East
Air Koryo has added the An-148 to revitalise its regional fleet. It is possible to travel on them only as part of a specially-arranged aviation tour of North Korea, such as those offered by Juche Travel Services.

Central & South America
Cubana are the sole operator of the An-158, based at Havana and operating domestic flights plus regional routes to Central America.

Beechcraft 18

One of the most numerous transport aircraft ever built, the Beechcraft Model 18 was built between 1937 and 1969 and saw service all over the world in civilian and military roles. The vast majority were used during World War II.

Today most are in museums or have been scrapped, but a precious few offer scenic charter flights for enthusiasts to enjoy.

Africa
Springbok Classic Air in Johannesburg, South Africa, fly a number of classic aircraft on scenic tours.

See **www.springbokclassicair.co.za**

USA & Canada
Vintage Aircraft in Stockton, California offer scenic flights and training in their Beech 18.

See **www.twinbeech.com**

Beechcraft 99

© Hector Rivera

Developed as an early commuter turboprop based on the Beech King Air and Queen Air aircraft, the Beech 99 saw moderate success around the world.

Today the remaining examples are mostly in service as package freighters feeding smaller airports, particularly in the USA, Canada and Caribbean. A few passenger examples can be found.

Caribbean

Flamingo Air in the Bahamas and **Hummingbird Air**, based at St. Croix in the US Virgin Islands, both offer scheduled and charter air taxi services with their Beech 99s.

InterCaribbean Airways flies three Beech 99s at the last count, based at Providenciales in the Turk & Caicos Islands. It flies local and regional scheduled services.

USA & Canada

North-Wright Airways serves remote communities out of Norman Wells, NWT, Canada, using a mixed fleet of light aircraft and turboprops, including two Beechcraft 99s.

Boeing 717-200

Inherited by Boeing when it merged with McDonnell Douglas, the 717 was originally designed as the MD-95 – the next in the long family line of DC-9 and MD-80 series aircraft which had developed since the 1960s.

Being so different from any other Boeing aircraft at the time, only moderate effort was put into sales of the type, and only 156 were built.

Whilst most of the built aircraft are still in service, few airlines fly the type. They are listed here.

Europe

Volotea Airlines operates the 717 on its scheduled and charter flights scattered all over southern Europe – particularly in France, Italy and Spain. It is slowly replacing the type with Airbus A320 family aircraft.

USA & Canada

Delta Airlines has the largest fleet of Boeing 717s in the world, operating out of Atlanta, Georgia, New York La Guardia and some other hubs, mainly on domestic routes. It inherited its fleet from AirTran Airways.

Hawaiian Airways operates 717s on domestic services around the Hawaiian Islands chain.

Oceania & Pacific

Qantas Link branded 717s are operated by Cobham Aviation Services around Australia, principally out of Melbourne and Sydney airports.

Boeing 727-200

Boeing reputedly saw what Hawker Siddeley were designing with their Trident, and what the Sud Aviation Caravelle had achieved, and set about designing their own T-tail, rear engine airliner. It went on to break all sales records, with its good operating performance and economies. Once seen in abundance all over the world, the 727 is now quite a rare sight.

No passenger-carrying examples of the shorter 727-100 model remain in service, however there are still some of the longer -200 models operating with cargo airlines, and only one passenger airline.

Number built: 1,260`

Asia & Middle East

The last operator of the type in the world, is **Iran Aseman Airlines**, who have three examples in service. They fly domestic and regional flights.

Interestingly some enthusiasts have managed to arrange flights on VIP-configured Boeing 727s recently. It is worth keeping an eye out for such opportunities.

Boeing 737-200

© Biggerben

Boeing 737 'Classics' (the -100 to -500 range) were developed from the late 1960s until the 1990s. Whilst all -100s are retired, and the -200 is a dying breed, the -300, -400, and -500 are still flying in sufficient numbers to be deemed unnecessary to cover in this book.

Here we look at the remaining 737-200s in passenger service. What was so prevalent in Europe and North America in the 1970s and 80s, and still very evident in Asia in the 2000s, is now quite rare.

Africa

Air Zimbabwe operates its vintage aircraft on the Harare-Johannesburg, South Africa route.

Central & South America

Aero Patagonia is a new airline based in Argentina. Little is known of its operations, however at least one 737-200 is registered to the airline in passenger configuration.

Avior Airlines, based at Barcelona in Venezuela, operates five examples in a smart new livery.

EasySky is a relatively new airline based at Golson International, La Ceiba, Honduras. It operates a single 737-200 and has plans to add Next Generation 737s in the near future.

Peruvian Airlines has two 737-200s in its fleet, flying domestic services from Lima.

USA & Canada

Air North based in Whitehorse, Yukon, has one example left flying. It operates as a mixed passenger-cargo Combi, flying to remote communities.

Air Inuit still operates two examples of the 737-200 on scheduled services out of Montreal to remote communities in the north of the country.

Candian North has the largest fleet of -200s of the Canadian airlines. Again, these fly passenger charters and schedules to remote communities, mostly from Edmonton, Iqaluit and Yellowknife.

Norlinor operates the type on charters from Montreal, often to gravel airstrips.

Boeing 737-600

When the Next Generation models of 737 emerged, they loosely matched the Classic predecessors. The 737-600 was a match for the -500, however it did little to stir sales interest from airlines. The largest operator was (and still is) Scandinavian Airlines. A few other airlines still fly this rarer variant.

Africa

Air Algerie seems to still fly at least four examples of the -600 from its Algiers base. They often fly into Europe.

Algeria's neighbour **Tunis Air** has a seven-strong fleet of -600s flying from Tunis to cities in Europe and Africa.

Europe

SAS Scandinavian Airlines is now the only operator of the type in Europe, however they still operate a sizeable fleet of Boeing 737-600s on routes around Scandinavia and into Europe. It is difficult to plan a flight as the different variants of 737s flown by the airline seem to be intermixed on many routes. The type is likely to be phased out from 2019.

USA & Canada

WestJet operate a fleet of 13 737-600s on domestic services within Canada. As newer 737 MAX aircraft are delivered the type is likely to be retired.

Boeing 747-300

© Paul Denton

Of the classic Boeing 747 models (-100, -200, -300 and SP), the -300 is now the only one with a chance of being flown on as a passenger.

The first Boeing 747 to feature a stretched upper deck (some -100s and -200s were retrofitted and classified SUD models), the -300 had a higher capacity but lacked the advancements soon to be seen in the -400 model. Only 81 were built.

Asia & Middle East

Mahan Air of Iran is now the last operator in the world of the 747-300, with a single example EP-MND. It is only a matter of time before newer aircraft replace the type completely. It is difficult to plan a flight on the 747 as the airline often mixes up the types it uses on different routes. Mostly this -300 has been operating domestic routes.

Boeing 757-300

Compared to the high-selling original 757-200 model, the stretched -300 variant seemed to only attract a few operators who found a niche role for it. Of these were primarily US scheduled airlines and European leisure operators.

A number are still going strong, and can be flown here:

Europe

Arkia of Israel operates two Boeing 757-300s from Tel Aviv Ben Gurion airport. Common routes include Eilat, Porto, Heraklion, Larnaca, Rhodes, Amsterdam and Kiev.

Condor fly from Manchester, UK and destinations in Germany to various holiday destinations in Europe with their fleet of 757-300s as part of the Thomas Cook Airways brand (along with two Thomas Cook Airlines UK examples). Usually only bookable as part of a package holiday, careful planning may bag a flight on the type.

Icelandair still flies a single example, TF-FIX, on a variety of services out of Reykjavik.

USA & Canada

Delta Airlines and **United Airlines** both operate fleets of Boeing 757-300s on scheduled domestic services across the country. Interestingly both airlines inherited these aircraft from mergers with Northwest Airlines and Continental Airlines respectively.

Boeing 767-200

The original Boeing 767 variant has become rarer in service with passenger airlines, whilst the -300 and, to some extent the -400, soldier on in decent numbers. Here are your chances to fly the shorter model.

Africa

Air Zimbabwe has one active 767-200, however the destinations served by the airline have been significantly reduced following bans.

Asia & Middle East

Safi Airways operate a sole example, YA-AQS, on routes from Kabul, Afghanistan to other destinations in Asia and the Middle East, including Dubai.

Europe

Meridiana operate a sole example, I-AIGH, alongside its 767-300s on various routes.

UTair operate a fleet of three Boeing 767-200s on various domestic routes in Russia from its base at Moscow Vnukovo.

USA & Canada

Omni Air International do not operate scheduled services, but mostly military charters and occasional ad-hoc flights on behalf of other airlines. They operate two examples, N207AX and N225AX.

British Aerospace ATP

The BAe ATP was intended as a competitor to the already well-covered commuter turboprop market. It was built as an extended and upgraded version of the popular HS./BAe 748 aircraft and first flew in 1986.

It was intended that a further development of the ATP would be added as the Jetstream 61, but the project was cancelled.

Europe

NextJet of Sweden is the only operator in the world now of the BAe ATP, with four aircraft. They are flown on various domestic flights in Sweden, mostly from Stockholm Arlanda.

British Aerospace 146

The 1980s era British four-engine airliner was developed in three variants, the -100, -200 and -300. From 1992 a modified airliner named the Avro RJ superseded the original models, being produced as the RJ70, RJ85 and RJ100. Attempts to further revitalise the series with the Avro RJX stalled in 2002 and no more aircraft were built.

BAe 146-100

The original model of the four-engine British airliner is the Bae 146-100. It is also one of the rarest with so few being built. Production started in 1983.

Asia & Middle East
SkyJet in the Philippines flies three BAe 146-100s exclusively on domestic services from Manila to Basco, Caticlan, Coron and Siargao.

Central & South America
Star Peru, based at Lima, operates two -100s alongside -200s and -300s on its domestic route network. Finding a flight on this variant will be largely down to luck.

BAe 146-200

Asia & Middle East
Aviastar is a small airline based in Jakarta, Indonesia, using Twin Otters and BAe 146-200s on domestic and government subsidy flights around the country.

Central & South America
Star Peru (see 146-100) have five examples.

Europe
Cello Aviation in the UK operate a sole example G-RAJJ on charters.

Similarly, Southend-based **JOTA Aviation** operate a single example G-SMLA, which often shows up as a substitute for scheduled services and charter flights.

WDL Aviation operate a sole example, again usually on charter services on behalf of other carriers. The airline is based in Cologne Bonn.

BAe 146-300

Asia & Middle East
Mahan Air of Iran owns one of the largest fleets of BAe 146-300s still flying. These operate domestic routes from Tehran Mehrabad.

Central & South America
Star Peru (see 146-100) complements its 146 fleet with two -300 variants.

Europe
Astra Airlines of Greece operates regional services from Thessaloniki with a single 146-300.

WDL Aviation operate a sole example, which is wet leased to various operaors.

British Aerospace/Avro RJ85

Moving on to the second generation of 146, branded as the Avro

RJ. No RJ70s fly in passenger service, but RJ85 and RJ100 operators can be flown with fairly easily.

Africa

SA Airlink based as Johannesburg and operating feeder flights on behalf of South African Airways. It operated over ten RJ85s alongside Jetstream and Embraer types.

Asia & Middle East

Mahan Air (see 146-300) uses some RJ85s on domestic routes.

Central & South America

Bolivia's **EcoJet** is a small regional airline operating out of Cochabamba. It has four RJ85s.

Europe

BRA Braathens Regional Airlines of Sweden supplements its ATR 72 and Saab 2000 fleets with a RJ85 used on domestic routes within Sweden.

Cityjet based in Dublin, with a large presence at London City Airport, supported airlines such as Air France for many years. Now they operate many flights on their own right, and recently pledged to keep some RJ85 and RJ100 fleets flying a little longer beyond the initial 2018 retirement date.

Ellinair of Thessaloniki in Greece flies two RJ85s alongside its Airbus and Boeing fleets. As well as scheduled services it sometimes supports holiday and leisure services in the summer.

JOTA Aviation (see 146-200) operates the RJ85 on ad-hoc charter services for other airlines.

USA & Canada

Summit Air based in Yellowknife, NWT, uses a single RJ85 on its charter services to remote communities. It does not offer scheduled services.

British Aerospace/Avro RJ100

Asia & Middle East

Mahan Air (see 146-300) flies RJ100s on domestic services from Tehran.

Caribbean

BVI Airways recently introduced two RJ100s for services between the British Virgin Islands and Miami, as well as some regional destinations.

Europe

BRA Braathens Regional Airlines (see RJ85) inherited ten RJ100s from its former identity as Malmo Aviation, operating domestic services in Sweden. Their main operating base is Stockholm Bromma Airport.

Brussels Airlines has a long history of operating BAe 146 and Avro RJ aircraft. Sadly, their feet will be retired in late 2017/ early 2018.

JOTA Aviation (see 146-200) uses RJ100 G-JOTS on charter work.

USA & Canada

North Cariboo Air uses two RJ100s on charter work, usually from its Calgary and Edmonton bases.

Summit Air (see RJ85) also uses a RJ100 aircraft.

Britten Norman BN-2 Islander

© JJ Harrison

Over 1,200 BN-2 Islanders and Trislanders were built by the small company based on the Isle of Wight, England, since it was introduced in 1965. The type is still being produced in Romania in small numbers.

Recently the BN-2T Trislander was retired by enthusiast-favourite Aurigny Air Services in the Channel Islands.

BN-2 Islanders are still flown in passenger service in a few locations.

Caribbean

Air Flamenco is the world's largest operator of Islanders, with ten examples. It flies short trips between Culebra in Puerto Rico and the Leedward Islands and Dominican Republic.

Divi Divi Air of Willemstad in Curaçao has three Islanders in its fleet. Its main operation is a regular service between Curaçao and Bonaire.

FlyMontserrat links the island with Antigua, Barbuda and Nevis using two Islanders.

Trans Anguilla Airways flies two BN2 Islanders between Anguilla and Sint Maarten, flying over the famous beach.

Vieques Air Link of Puerto Rico uses Islanders and Trislanders on short domestic hops around the island.

Windward Express Airways is based at Sint Maarten and flies two Islanders mostly on charter work to nearby islands and destinations.

Europe

Aer Arran Islands, a spin off from the original Aer Arann, which now operates as Stobart Air/Aer Lingus Regional, uses the Islander on island-hopping flights from Connemara Airport. It is expected to replace the services with helicopters in the near future.

Hebridean Air Services use two Islanders for air ambulance, charter and some scheduled flights around the Scottish Highlands and Islands.

Isles of Scilly Skybus uses a fleet of Islanders and Twin Otters to link the remote Scilly Isles with airports in mainland United Kingdom such as Exeter, Lands End and Newquay.

Loganair utilises the Islands on island-hopping flights in Scotland – particularly in the Orkney and Shetland Islands.

Oceania & Pacific

Anyone visiting Tasmania could get a trip on a BN2 Islander operated by **Airlines of Tasmania** (often known as Par-Avion), which flies scenic flights and charters with the type from Hobart.

Barrier Air and **Fly My Sky** are two competing airlines operating out of Auckland International Airport. Both fly the BN2 Islander on short hops and sightseeing flights.

Torres Strait Air is based at Horn Island of Queensland's northern coast and uses the Islander for short flights to airstrips around the Torres Strait.

USA & Canada

Cape Air is a regional airline linking smaller communities around New England. It operates four Islander aircraft as part of its fleet, which tend to fly in the Caribbean during the winter months.

Convair 440/580

The Convair CV-580 was part of the CV-240 family. It came about as a conversion of the CV-340 or CV-440 aircraft, giving it turboprop engines and other improvements. A small number are still in passenger configuration.

Oceania & Pacific

Air Chathams of New Zealand's remote island group still flies commercially with several Convair 580s. They have been used regularly on the link from Auckland to the islands, but predicting the schedule is difficult.

USA & Canada

Norlinor, based at Montreal, operate a single CV-440 and a single CV-580. Both are used on charter services, so would need to be chartered. At least one enthusiast group has organised this in the past.

de Havilland DH.89 Dragon Rapide

Built in the 1930s as a state-of-the-art passenger airliner, the Dragon Rapide today is an example of the glory days of flying. Over 700 were built, and a number are still flying and available for experience flights.

Europe

Classic Wings offers pleasure flights in two of its eight-seater Dragon Rapides from the Imperial War Museum, Duxford, UK. These pleasure flights mostly operate during the summer season on weekends and Wednesdays.

de Havilland DH.104 Dove

An art-deco airliner developed just after World War 2, the DH.104 Dove is one of Britain's most successful airliners. It acted as a feeder airliner for carriers, and also enjoyed service as a military transport aircraft (called the Devon). A number remain with preservation organisations.

Europe

LTU Classic in Germany regularly flies its two Dove aircraft on the airshow circuit, and organises pleasure flights in them.

Find out more at **www.ltu-classic.de**

de Havilland DH.114 Heron

Following on from the DH.104 Dove, the DH.114 Heron came along in 1950 and offered increased capacity through a stretch of the fuselage. It featured four piston engines and the same art deco style of the smaller airliner.

Europe

Vasteras Flygmuseum Riley in Sweden have a beautifully restored Heron, registration N415SA, which operates occasional scenic charter flights from its base at Vasteras Airport west of Stockholm. See **www.hasslo.org** for more information.

de Havilland Canada DHC-6 Twin Otter

© Timo Breidenstein

Over 900 DHC-6 Twin Otters were produced between 1965 and 1988 when the original run ended. In recent years Viking Air has resurrected the type, producing the DHC-6-400 series, offering modern avionics and new engines. Clearly there is still a market for such a type, and many types of organisation still fly them around the world for different purposes.

For the enthusiast looking to fly on a Twin Otter, including the modern variant, the options are as follows:

Africa

Air Seychelles uses its fleet of DHC-6-400s to ferry passengers from the international airport at Mahe to smaller airports around the island chain.

Maldivian has ten DHC-6-300s flying tourists to resorts around the Maldives from the international airport.

Trans Maldivian Airways has over 40 seaplane Twin Otters in its fleet, including some modern Viking examples. It flies tourists to resorts on the Maldives from the international airport.

Asia & Middle East

Aviastar is a small airline based in Jakarta, Indonesia, using Twin Otters and BAe 146-200s on domestic and government subsidy flights around the country.

MASwings is a small regional airline operating out of Kota Kinabalu and Kuching to airports in the east of Malaysia.

Nepal Airlines uses three Twin Otters. You may experience these on flights to Lukla, near Everest.

Tara Air focuses on serving remote communities with its fleet of STOL aircraft, including the Twin Otter. It is based at Kathmandu, Nepal.

Trigana Air Service uses DHC-6-300s on short domestic routes in Indonesia.

Caribbean

SVG Air flies its Twin Otter fleet around airports in the Caribbean from its base at Argyle Airport in St Vincent and the Grenadines.

Winair is based at Sint Maarten. Its DHC-6-300s flies regularly between islands in the Leeward and Antilles chains.

Europe
Isles of Scilly Skybus uses Twin Otters alongside its Britten Norman Islanders to link the Scilly Isles with the mainland airports of Exeter, Newquay and Lands End.

Loganair still flies one classic DHC-6-300 and is replacing the fleet with newer Viking Twin Otters. These are used on flights from Glasgow to Scottish islands, including the famous beach runway at Barra.

Nordic Seaplanes is an interesting operator flying a DHC-6 between Copenhagen and Aarhus harbours.

Norlandair, based at Akureyri in Iceland, flies DHC-6-300s on three domestic routes.

Oceania & Pacific
Air Vanuatu is replacing its Harbin Y-12s with three Twin Otters for local island services.

Aircalin of New Caledonia flies local services with two Twin Otters from the main airport at Noumea.

Fiji Link flies feeder links for its parent airline Fiji Airways around these Pacific islands from a base at Nadi International Airport.

Polynesian Airlines provides links around Samoa using Twin Otters from the main airport at Apia.

Solomon Airlines feeds passengers from Honiara International to other smaller islands in the chain using DHC-6-300s.

USA & Canada

Air Inuit, based at Montreal, Canada, flies DHC-6's and other types on scheduled and charter services to remote communities.

Air Labrador is a regional scheduled airliner with eight Twin Otters used on routes throughout Newfoundland and Labrador. It is based at Goose Bay.

Air Tindi is based at Yellowknife airport, flying Twin Otters on scheduled and charter services.

Grand Canyon Airlines based at Boulder City, Nevada (near Las Vegas) flies its Twin Otters on scenic flights to and over the Grand Canyon.

Provincial Airlines (PAL Airlines) flies scheduled, charter and air ambulance services throughout Labrador and Newfoundland in north east Canada. It has bases at St. John's, Goose Bay, Montreal and Halifax. Its Twin Otter fleet is six-strong.

de Havilland Canada DHC-7

The "Dash 7" was developed in the early 1970s to provide an airliner which has STOL (Short Take-Off and Landing) capabilities, allowing it to operate into the shortest runways and landing strips. It incorporated many of the design features of the popular DHC-6 Twin Otter, and was also vastly quieter than most other airliners at the time. Only 113 examples were built, however, as the type failed to make a dent into the market occupied by types such as the Fokker F27 and Hawker Siddeley 748.

Africa

Airkenya Express based at Nairobi uses two Dash 7 aircraft on domestic flights and its link to Kilimanjaro in Tanzania.

USA & Canada

Air Tindi uses its five Dash 7 aircraft to fly combined cargo and passenger services to outlying communities, making use of its ability to land on unprepared strips. Its bases are at Fort Simpson and Yellowknife airports.

Voyageur Airways of North Bay, Ontario, has a fleet of three Dash 7s. It only flies charter work, however.

Dornier 328

The Dornier 328 was a twin-turboprop airliner which first flew in 1991 and aimed to take a chunk of the market for regional aircraft at the time. It achieved moderate success, with just over 200 frames being built before production ceased in 2000.

With the acquisition of Dornier by Fairchild in 1996, a second variant of the aircraft was also developed. Named the Fairchild Dornier 328JET it had, as the name suggests, jet engines instead of turboprops on essentially the same body.

Recent developments have worked towards resurrecting the aircraft by Turkish Aerospace Industries which would see it renamed the TRJ-328 – again as both a jet and turboprop aircraft. Modified Dornier examples are serving as prototypes ahead of production beginning.

Dornier 328-100

Central & South America
ADA Aerolinea de Antioquia has three Dornier 328-100s in its fleet. It flies domestic routes within Colombia, based in Medellin.

Europe
Loganair has a fleet of three Dornier 328-100s turboprop examples from its Scottish hubs on routes around the United Kingdom. Until recently these aircraft operated in Flybe livery, but will no doubt wear Loganair's colours now that the partnership is ending.

MHS Aviation/Rhein-Neckar Air is a small German regional airline operating Dornier 328 flights between Mannheim and Berlin, as well as on charter work.

Skywork Airlines operates a small fleet of 328-100s on routes from Bern and Basel in Switzerland. They are expected to be retired imminently.

Sun Air of Scandinvaia operates a fleet of Dornier 328-100s from its Billund base in Denmark. These aircraft operate in British Airways livery.

Fairchild Dornier 328JET

Central & South America
FlyMex operates two 328JETs on charter services out of Toluca, Mexico.

Europe

Sun Air of Scandinavia (see 328-100). Some of their 15 JET examples are again painted in British Airways colours, flying routes out of Billund. Others fly for the **JoinJet** VIP service.

USA & Canada

Calm Air of Canada flies two Dornier 328JETs on charter services, sometimes on behalf of other carriers.

Key Lime Air based at Denver Centennial Airport operates its Dornier 328JETs on shuttle services around Colorado and Wyoming, as well as charter work.

Ultimate Air Shuttle operates VIP charter services which can be booked by the public. It operates out of Cincinnati, Ohio, using eight 328JET aircraft, serving cities such as Atlanta, Charlotte, Chicago, Cleveland and New York, mostly using secondary airports.

Douglas DC-3/C-47

By far one of the best-known airliners ever produced, and certainly amongst the most numerous ever built (albeit largely for military transport purposes in the C-47 guise), the DC-3 'Dakota' has a special place in many enthusiasts' hearts. A flight in an airworthy example is seen as the classic airliner every enthusiast must fly on at least once. Thankfully many examples still fly around the world, and we list many of the known operators here.

Africa

Skyclass Aviation at Rand, Johannesburg, uses DC-3 ZS-BXF for airshows and sightseeing flights, alongside its DC-4. See **www.flyskyclass.com**

Europe

Aero Passion / Breitling operate DC-3 HB-IRJ alongside their Lockheed Constellation aircraft. Roundtrips for members are available when the aircraft is not undertaking other duties. Based in Switzerland.

Dakota Norway operates LN-WND from Sandefjord Torp airport, with flights available. See **www.dakotanorway.no**

DC Association in Finland maintain and operated the immaculate DC-3 OH-LCH in Finnair livery. It flies members of the association. See **www.dc-ry.fi**

The Dutch Dakota Association in Holland operates DDA Airlines from Amsterdam Schiphol airport. They have two DC-3s which operate regularly, taking passengers who can book through their website at **www.dutchdakota.nl**

First Austrian DC-3 Dakota Club uses a 'vistaliner' DC-3 with enlarged windows for scenic flights. The aircraft, N86U, wears vintage Austrian Airlines colours and is based at Salzburg. See **www.dc-3.club** for information on events and flight opportunities.

Flygande Veteraner has a beautiful DC-3 in classic Scandinavian Airlines colours based at Stockholm Bromma airport in Sweden and offering flights. See **www.flygandeveteraner.se**

Oceania & Pacific

Air Chathams is the chief operator based in the Chatham Islands off New Zealand. Their DC-3 ZK-AWP is actually based at Auckland International and is available for scenic charter flights.

Fly DC3 NZ operates scenic flights to a schedule from Ardmore Airport near Auckland, New Zealand in a 1940s DC-3.
See **www.flydc3.co.nz**

Melbourne Gooney Bird offers scenic flights around its home base at Melbourne Essendon Airport, including dinner flights.
See **www.melbournesgooneybird.com.au**

USA & Canada

Aerometal International of Aurora, Oregon, are dedicated to maintaining classic aircraft. They offer flight training on the DC-3.
See **www.aerometalinternational.com**

Buffalo Airways until recently were the last airline offering scheduled service by DC-3. However its flights between Yellowknife and Hay River are not operating at present. There may still be some passenger opportunities with the airline's DC-3s, however.

Flagship Detroit Foundation preserves one of the best-known flying DC-3s wearing the colours of American Airlines. NC17334 is based at Fort Worth Meacham airport in Texas, but appears at shows all over the country. Flights are available.
See **www.flagshipdetroit.org**

Golden Age Air Tours based in Sonoma, California, north of San Francisco, operate N341A on scenic flights.
See **www.goldenageairtours.com**

Skydive Skyranch in Siloam Spring, Arkansas, recently started offering skydiving from its own DC-3 aircraft.
See **www.skyranch.com**

Vintage Flying Museum in Fort Worth, Texas, has an immaculate DC-3 painted in the colours it wore during World War II service. Rides are available.
See **www.vintageflyingmuseum.org**

Wings of Valor based in Perris, California, operate NC43XX in Thunderbird Flying Service colours on scenic flights. Minimum number of passengers apply.
See **www.wingsofvalor.net**

The Yankee Air Museum at Detroit Willow Run Airport, Michigan, offers rides in its DC-3 aircraft. They often operate from other locations, so check their website at **www.yankeeairmuseum.org**

Douglas DC-4

© Steve Brimley

The famous four-engined piston airliner built to complement the successful DC-3. It famously took part in the Berlin Airlift, and many more military versions (designated C-54) were built than passenger examples.

Sadly few chances to fly one in passenger service exist.

Africa

Skyclass Aviation operate ZS-AUB and ZS-BMH with stylish interior layouts. They are held at the SAA Museum at Rand Airport near Johannesburg, South Africa. Alongside their DC-3, flights in the DC-4 are regularly offered at special events.

See their website for details **www.saamuseum.co.za**

Douglas DC-9

© Guido Potters

The original DC-9 model was the shorter -10 series, which actually comprised the -11, -12, -13, -14, and -15 variants. Each had slightly different specifications. The most numerous of these were the -14 and -15. Delta Air Lines was the original operator of the DC-9 (and thus the -10 model).

The DC-9-20 series was only a niche model built to give SAS an aircraft that could operate out of short field runways, using the fuselage of -10 model. Only 20 of the type were built.

The most popular DC-9 variant was the -30, which enjoyed service with many airlines around the world and was a worthy rival for Boeing's popular 737. It entered service in 1967.

The final steps in DC-9 design before the McDonnell Douglas MD-80 series were the DC-9-40 and -50 variants, with longer fuselages and greater capacity, operated by the likes of Eastern Airlines, Delta, Finnai, Swissair and Northwest Airlines.

Africa

African Express Airways has been using a single DC-9-30 on routes from its Nairobi Wilson base.

Fly-SAX of Kenya operates the oldest flying DC-9 aircraft, both -10 models, also from Nairbo Wilson airport on regional and domestic routes.

Central & South America

Venezuela's **LASER** airlines has a number of DC-9-31s in its fleet, but have reportedly been stored pending reactivation or scrapping. Worth keeping an eye on.

USA & Canada

Skydive Perris famously used the only flying DC-9-20 as a parachute drop platform out of its Perris, California base. It is reportedly looking into reactivating this aircraft.

See **www.skydiveperris.com**

Embraer 120 Brasilia

© Eugene Butler

Following on from the 110 Bandeirante, Embraer developed its next twin-turboprop commuter airliner which was aimed at feeder airlines all over the world. Over 350 were built, including some military variants, until production ceased in 2001.

Africa-DTL Air Charters in South Africa, they have a single example- ZS-TBF. Majestic

Caribbean
InterCaribbean Airways has a growing fleet of Brasilias operating from its base at Providenciales, Turks & Caicos. The airline flies to many Caribbean islands.

Central & South America
Brava Linhas Aereas of Porto Alegre, Brazil, is using a single Brasilia on domestic services. It plans to add more.

Piquiatuba Transportes Aereos is another Brazilian domestic airline using the Brasilia. It is based at Santarem in northern Brazil.

Oceania & Pacific
Airnorth of Darwin, Australia, uses five aircraft alongside ERJ-170s on domestic routes.

USA & Canada
Great Lakes Airlines now flies solely under its own branding and flight numbers, having operated as a United Express feeder for many years. It flies EMB-120 Brasilias out of Denver International.

Key Lime Air, based at Denver Centennial Airport, has a single Brasilia in its fleet for scheduled services in Colorado and Wyoming.

Fairchild Swearingen Metro

This versatile twin turboprop airliner came in many different varieties, usually labelled a Metro Metroliner or Merlin. Its thin, pencil-like fuselage was popular with regional feeder airliners, and it has become a popular cargo carrier in later life.

The few known operators to offer scheduled services with the type are as follows.

Europe

North Flying is a Danish operator with four Metroliners in its fleet. It does not offer scheduled services, but often uses its aircraft on charters and sub-contracts to other airlines.

USA & Canada

Bearskin Airlines, based at Thunder Bay, Ontario, uses a number of 19 seat Metro aircraft of different varieties. They operate within Ontario and Manitoba.

Perimeter Aviation of Winnipeg, Canada, has a varied mix of uses for its aircraft, which include around 25 Metros and Merlins capable of carrying passengers. Some scheduled services are offered around Manitoba and Ontario.

Fokker 50

Developed out of the success of the Fokker F27 airliner, the Fokker 50 first flew in 1985 and was produced until 1997 after 213 examples had been built. It was a popular regional airliner and quite common to see particularly in Europe.

Numbers are now dwindling, so it's time to try one before the numbers reduce further.

Africa
Jetways Airlines uses three Fokker 50s on domestic charter and scheduled flights from Nairobi Wilson airport in Kenya.

Jubba Airways of Kenya uses one Fokker 50 among other aircraft for flights to Djibouti and Somalia.

Ocean Airlines uses Fokker 50s on scheduled services from destinations around Somalia, plus regional routes to Nairobi and Djibouti.

Skyward Express is a small Kenyan airline flying daily between Nairobi and Mombasa. It has two Fokker 50s.

Asia & Middle East
Aero Mongolia, based at Ulaanbaatar flies three Fokker 50s on domestic routes, and some services into Russia and Hohhot in China.

Iranian Naft Airlines uses five Fokker 50s on domestic and regional services from Ahwaz Airport.

Caribbean
Insel Air of Curaçao and Aruba have a few Fokker 50s in their fleet, flying to destinations around the Caribbean.

Central & South America
Air Panama flies regional services from Panama City to destinations in Panama and neighbouring countries. It has a small fleet of Fokker 50s.

Avior Regional, part of Avior Airlines in Venezuela, use Fokker 50s on domestic services within the country.

Oceania & Pacific

Alliance Airlines uses Fokker 50s mostly on mining operations, but also can be used on its limited scheduled services.

Fokker 70

Developed alongside the Fokker 100 as a replacement for the F28 aircraft, the Fokker 70 was the smaller variant, aimed at regional routes. Only 48 were built, but the type has survived as a reliable and popular aircraft with both airlines and passengers.

The largest operator of the type, KLM Cityhopper, is retiring its fleet by November 2017 and therefore is not listed here. Most of its aircraft have been sold on to other carriers.

Asia & Middle East

Air KBZ of Myanmar, is taking two used Fokker 70s on domestic routes from Yangon and Mandalay airports.

Caribbean

Insel Air of Aruba and Curaçao utilises the Fokker 70 on flights around the Caribbean.

Central & South America

Fly All Ways, the strangely-named airline from Suriname, uses two Fokker 70s on flights from Paramaribo to Brazil, Barbados, Sing Maarten and Curaçao.

Europe

Austrian Airlines has held on to its Fokker fleet for a long time, but these are to be retired in 2018. Catch one while you can!

Oceania & Pacific

Air Nuigini, the national airline of Papua New Guinea, is utilising nine second-hand Fokker 70s to supplement its fleet of Fokker 100s and larger Boeing 737s. These operate domestic routes, and some regional flights to Australia.

Alliance Airlines is solely a Fokker operator, with 50 and 100 models in its fleet alongside its 70s. Although much of its operation is focused around the mining industry in Western Australia, the airline has some scheduled routes from Perth, Adelaide and Cairns.

Fokker 100

The largest of the Fokker aircraft. Built between 1986 and 1997, with 283 airframes completed.

Africa

IRS Airlines, based in Abuja, Nigeria, uses a fleet of Fokker 100s for scheduled domestic services.

Jetways Airlines uses Fokker 100s on domestic charter and scheduled flights from Nairobi Wilson airport in Kenya.

Ocean Airlines uses Fokker 100s on scheduled services from destinations around Somalia, plus regional routes to Nairobi and Djibouti.

Asia & Middle East

Caspiy is a small airline in Kazakhstan flying Fokker 100s between Almaty and Uralsk.

Iran Air once had a large fleet of Fokker 100s. It has somewhat reduced to four at the time of writing, and will likely reduce completely in the near future.

Iran Aseman Airlines uses Fokker 100s on domestic routes.

Iranian Naft Airlines flies four of the type domestically and regionally from Ahwaz.

Kish Air has two Fokker 100s based at Kish Island in Iran.

Qeshm Airlines of Iran uses four Fokker 100s on domestic services.

- Kish Air, Iranian Naft Airlines, Nafi Air.

Central & South America

Air Panama flies regional services from Panama City to destinations in Panama and neighbouring countries. It has a small fleet of Fokker 100s.

Europe

Austrian Airlines still uses Fokker 100s, but these are being replaced by Embraer 195s and will not remain into 2018.

Carpatair of Romania operate two examples on charters, having ceased flying its own scheduled services.

Helvetic Airlines operates four Fokker 100s on behalf of Swiss International Air Lines. They are likely to be phased out in favour of more Embraer 195s soon.

Trade Air has two Fokker 100s, used mostly on charter flights on behalf of other carriers. Based at Zagreb, Croatia.

Oceania & Pacific

Air Nuigini, the national airline of Papua New Guinea, is utilising Fokker 100s alongside larger Boeing 737s. These operate domestic routes, and some regional flights to Australia.

Alliance Airlines uses Fokker 100s alongside Fokker 50s and 70s. The airline has some scheduled routes from Perth, Adelaide and Cairns.

QantasLink has 17 Fokker 100s which are operated by Network Aviation. They can be flown domestically from most major hubs and airports, particularly in eastern Australia.

Virgin Australia Regional Airlines, formerly Skywest Airlines of Australia, has 15 Fokker 100s based in Perth, but with a network stretching across the country.

Ford Tri-Motor

© Gary Chambers

This small airliner was built from 1925 to 1933 and enjoyed sales around the world. However, many of the units built were for use as transports for military operators. The type was nicknamed the 'Tin Goose' due to its all-metal construction.

USA & Canada

The **Experimental Aircraft Association (EAA)** operates an example, NC8704, which they tour around the USA offering pleasure flights on. The EAA also offer pleasure flights at the annual EAA Air Adventure Air Show held at Oskhosh, Wisconsin, each summer.

Grumman G-21 Goose

A unique floating commuter airliner capable of flying from water locations around the world, yet with wheels to allow it to operate on land. The Grumman Goose has two large radial engines to the side of the bulbous cabin, mounted in high wings. Around 345 examples were built, finding work in the war effort and military organisations, as well as with civil operators. A number are still used by private owners today.

USA & Canada

Pacific Coastal Airlines uses Grumman Goose aircraft owned by Wilderness Seaplanes. They operate from Port Hardy, British Columbia, among other destinations.

The Goose Hangar in Anchorage, Alaska, operates Goose N703 to train pilots or give experiences in flying seaplanes. See **www.goosehangar.com**

Ilyushin IL-18

© Mark Fahey

One of the most successful airliners to emerge from the former Soviet Union, the Ilyushin IL-18 has stood the test of time. From its entry into service in 1957 to the present day, many carriers have used the type, despite jet aircraft emerging shortly after its introduction. Today, numbers are dwindling.

Asia & Middle East

Air Koryo of North Korea is the last commercial operator of the type. You can only fly on this aircraft if you are on an organised aviation tour of North Korea.

Ilyushin IL-62

© Weimeng

Russia's famed long-haul airliner from the 1960s is fading from our skies. Of the 292 examples built, only a few operators are left; these are mostly carrying cargo.

Europe

Rada Airlines of Belarus operates an Ilyushin IL-62, EW-450TR, in a mixed passenger-cargo configuration. It is usually available for charter work, and has appeared on at least one Belarus aviation tour offered by Merlintour.

Asia & Middle East

Air Koryo of North Korea is one of the last IL-62 operators. You can only fly on their aircraft by joining an organised aviation tour of North Korea.

Ilyushin IL-76

The cargo-carrying Ilyushin IL-76 was never really envisioned as a passenger aircraft. So flying on one has always been difficult. Nevertheless, there are tour companies who can organise flights on the type as part of packages they put together for special flight enthusiasts. The airlines they use include:

Asia & Middle East
Air Koryo of North Korea, as part of tours offered by companies such as Juche Travel Services.
See **www.juchetravelservices.com**

Europe
Ruby Star of Belarus, as part of tours offered by companies such as Merlintour.
See **www.merlintour.fr**

Ilyushin IL-96-300

© Paul Carlotti

Despite making its first flight in 1988 and entering service in 1992, the Ilyushin IL-96 is still in occasional production, even though original operators such as Aeroflot have retired the type. All new variants will be of the -400 variety, with reworked engines, which is being pushed as a Russian alternative for the prevalence of Airbus and Boeing types.

Central & South America

Cubana, Cuba's national carrier is at present the sole operator of this type. They operate examples on routes to Caracas, Venezuela, Paris-Orly, France and Madrid, Spain. It can be a challenge to arrange a flight on the IL-96, but worth the effort!

Ilyushin IL-114

© Igor Dvurekov

The Russian turboprop which had ambitions to replace the ageing Antonov An-24 family still in widespread used what the Ilyushin IL-114. It first flew in 1990, but did not enter service until 1998 due to technical issues and delays caused by the breakup of the USSR. Funding was eventually cancelled and only 20 aircraft were built.

Asia & Middle East

The only operator of the IL-114 is **Uzbekistan Airways**. The airline operates a fleet of five examples out of Tashkent on domestic services.

Junkers Ju 52

© Mario Serranò

One of the most numerous airliners built in Europe, the Junkers Ju 52 actually enjoyed more success in military transport roles than with airlines. It was built in Germany, France and Spain between 1931 and 1952, with a distinctive corrugated metal fuselage and three piston engines. Today a handful are maintained in flying condition as a tribute to this aircraft.

Europe

The appropriately named **Ju Air** in Switzerland flies three Ju 52s at the time of writing. They are available for pleasure flights from the company's base at Dübendorf.
See **www.ju-air.ch**

Lufthansa has a historic flight department which works on the restoration and operation of some iconic aircraft. Among them is Ju 52 D-AQUI which flies pleasure flights and roundtrips around Germany between April and October.
To book, see **www.dlbs.de/en**

Let L-410

One of the ugliest aircraft to have flown, yet one of Eastern Europe's more successful types, having been developed and built in Czechoslovakia (later the Czech Republic) from 1969. A modified 'Next Generation' variant is in production today.

Asia & Middle East

KrasAvia is one of Russia's largest regional carriers. Its route structure and timetable are difficult to navigate and plan. The airline does, nevertheess, operate a number of Let L-410s.

Sky Pasada operates L-410s from Manila's main airport to smaller Philippine destinations such as Basco, Itbayat, Palanan and Binalonan.

Summit Air (formerly Goma Air) is based at Kathmandu, Nepal, operating to domestic destinations. One of its L-410s was recently lost in a crash at Lukla.

Central & South America

Nature Air is one of Costa Rica's regional carriers, utilising a fleet of DHC-6 Twin Otters and Let L-410s from San Jose's main airport. Most destinations are domestic, with flights also operated to Panama and Managua.

SATENA is Colombia's government run airline. It flies domestic routes from main bases at Bogota and Medellin. Among the airline's varied fleet are three Let L-410s, usually flying between San Andres and Providencia.

Europe

Komiaviatrans is a small Russian regional carrier operating from Syktyvakar on a range of domestic routes. It operates L-410s and Embraer 145s.

Silver Air is a Czech airline which operates L-410s from the Italian island of Elba to domestic destinations. It also operates in Hungary, Romania and Switzerland.

Lisunov Li-2

© Julian Herzog

The license-built variant of the Douglas DC-3 was built in Moscow and later Tashkent to provide carriers and military organisations in this region with aircraft.

Over 6,000 examples were built before production ceased in 1952, however only one airworthy example is known to exist.

Europe

The **Goldtimer's Foundation** operate a sole example, HA-LIX, on pleasure flights from Buadors, Hungary.

See **www.goldtimer.hu**

Lockheed Super Constellation

© Alex Watts

Built at Burbank, California, the Lockheed Constellation became an iconic aircraft with its four radial engines and onboard luxury. Close to 1,000 examples were built over the four models, seeing service with most major airlines around the world, not to mention many air forces. A number are preserved today.

Europe

Super Constellation Flyers Association of Switzerland offer pleasure flights with their Lockheed Super Constellation, HB-RSC, in Breitling livery. You need to be a member of the Super Constellation Flyers Association for three months before you are eligible for a flight.

See **www.superconstellation.org**

McDonnell Douglas MD-80/90 series

Spawning from the successful Douglas DC-9 family (see earlier entry), the McDonnell Douglas MD-80 series of aircraft saw stretches in capacity, range and upgraded technology on board the aircraft. They proved successful with scheduled and leisure airlines the world over. However, in recent years the number of active MD-80s has dramatically reduced, to the point that they are included in this book as a dying breed!

MD-81

Central & South America

LASER of Venezuela appears to be the only remaining operator of the MD-81 variant. Its fleet are based at Caracas Simon Bolivar airport.

MD-82

Asia & Middle East

Far Eastern Air Transport has a long association with MD-80 series aircraft. It has five MD-82s in its fleet, flying domestic services in Taiwan.

Iran Air has four MD-82s to supplement its domestic fleet, but will likely replace them in the near future as modern types are delivered.

Iran Air Tours is a subsidiary of Iran Air. It uses MD-82s from Tehran, Mashhad and Shiraz on flights around Iran and the Middle East.

Kish Air fly MD-82s on internal routes within Iran, and on flights to Dubai, UAE, from its Kish Island base.

Zagros Airlines is another Iranian airlines flying both the MD-82 and -83 on domestic sectors from Tehran.

Caribbean

PAWA Dominicana is the main carrier of the Dominican Republic. It has a single MD-82 and some MD-83s which are used on services throughout the Caribbean. They are a common sight at Sint Maarten.

Central & South America
LASER airlines in Venezuela also operates the MD-82 on scheduled services.

Europe
ALK Airlines is a Bulgarian charter airline which operates two examples.

Bulgarian Air Charter operate a fleet of ten MD-82s on charters from Sofia and Varna to places such as Cologne and Dusseldorf in Germany, amongst other European destinations.

USA & Canada
American Airlines still operates the world's largest fleet of MD-82 aircraft. They are primarily based at Chicago O'Hare and Dallas Fort Worth airports and operate domestic services. The fleet is being retired in favour of Airbus and Boeing types at a fast pace.

MD-83

Asia & Middle East
ATA Airlines, based at Tabriz in Iran, flies MD-83s on domestic and regional flights.

Caspian Airlines uses a fleet of MD-83s on domestic and regional scheduled flights from Tehran Mehrabad, Iran.

Far Eastern Air Transport uses MD-83s alongside its MD-82s in Taiwan.

Kish Air (see MD-82) uses the MD-83 also on its scheduled services.

Zagros Airlines (see MD-82) based in Tehran.

Caribbean
PAWA Dominicana (see MD-82) flies four MD-83s on scheduled services.

Central & South America
Andes Lineas Aereas is an Argentinian regional airline. It flies MD-83s and -88s from Salta and Buenos Aires.

Europe
Bravo Airways based at Kiev Borispol in Ukraine uses several MD-83s on charter services throughout Eastern Europe.

UM Air similarly uses the MD-83 from Kiev to destinations throughout Eastern Europe and the CIS.

USA & Canada
Allegiant Air is still a significant operator of MD-83 aircraft, having taken a lot second-hand to develop its low-cost scheduled services throughout America. It flies particularly from secondary airports to major leisure hubs, such as Orlando and Las Vegas. It will continue operating their large fleet of MD-80s until around 2020.

American Airlines (see MD-82) operates substantial numbers of MD-83s on domestic trunk routes. They are being retired fast.

MD-88

Asia & Middle East
Iran's **Taban Air** a number of MD-88s out of its Mashhad base on domestic schedules.

USA & Canada
Allegiant Air operates eight examples on its low-cost scheduled services. They are due to be retired around 2020.

The main operator in North Amercia of the MD-88 is **Delta Airlines**, which has a sizeable fleet operating on various domestic routes from its hub at Atlanta, Georgia. Other good places to fly on one are from Washington Reagan National or New York La Guardia, Airports.

MD-90-30

USA & Canada
Delta Airlines operate a sizeable fleet on various routes in the United States. The airlines is now the only operator of the MD-90 in the world.

Saab 340

This Swedish-built commuter turboprop airliner was very popular with feeder and regional airlines around the world – particularly in Australia, Europe and the United States. Built over two variants, the 340A and 340B/B+, it would also later see the Saab 2000, which was a stretch of the original.

As the Saab aged the number of examples still flying passengers have dwindled.

Asia & Middle East

Hokkaido Air System uses three Saab 340s on regional flights out of Okadama Airport in Japan.

Japan Air Commuter still uses a fleet of nine Saab 340s for feeder flights out of Kagoshima and Osaka Kansai International airports to regional destinations around Japan.

Caribbean

Cayman Airways has a small fleet of Saabs to supplement larger aircraft used on its flights out of George Town, Grand Cayman.

Seaborne Airlines is based in San Juan, Puerto Rico. Its fleet comprises mostly Saab 340s, with destinations around the Caribbean.

SkyBahamas Airlines flies from various islands in the Bahamas, and also to Florida. It has two Saab 340s.

Western Air is based at Nassau in the Bahamas. It operates scheduled Saab 340 services to Florida, Jamaica, Haiti and other Caribbean destinations.

Europe

Loganair uses Saab 340s in both passenger and cargo configurations to operate domestic services around the UK, particularly from its Edinburgh, Glasgow, Inverness and Aberdeen bases.

Nextjet is a major regional airline from Sweden. Most of its flights are domestic services from Stocholm's Arlanda and Bromma airports, with some international routes to Helsinki. The Saab 340 makes up most of its fleet.

Sprint Air of Poland has Saab 340s in both freighter and 'quick change' variants, allowing it to fly passengers of the aircraft. The airline flies from Warsaw to destinations in Czech Republic and Ukraine.

Oceania & Pacific

Air Chathams Air Rarotonga uses a single Saab 340 among other aircraft. It usually operates the type from Rarotonga in the Cook Islands to Auckland International in New Zealand.

REX Regional Express is Australia's largest regional airline. It is based at Sydney airport, with outposts at most major airports. It operates over 50 Saab 340s, covering all three variants.

USA & Canada

Pacific Coastal Airlines is a commuter airline based in Vancouver. It has two Saab 340s operating to cities throughout British Columbia.

PenAir uses Saab 340s on regional feeder flights, particularly within Alaska from its Anchorage base. The aircraft also operate from Boston, Denver and Portland.

Silver Airways has a strong fleet of Saab 340s. It is based at Fort Lauderdale, Florida, serving airports throughout the state, and also many destinations in the Bahamas.

Transwest Air, based at Prince Albert, Saskatchewan, uses two Saabs for scheduled services around the region.

Saab 2000

The stretched version of the Saab 340 emerged in 1992, adding extra seats to the popular regional airliner. Only 63 were built, however, with most operated in Switzerland initially.

Today a number of small carriers use the type, so it's relatively easy to get a flight on one for the time being.

Europe

BRA Braathens Regional Airlines in Sweden uses Saab 2000s on domestic and regional links from its Stockholm Bromma base. It also leases two examples to Tus Airways (see below).

Darwin Airline (Etihad Regional) operate a small fleet on European services in Switzerland on behalf of Etihad. Two of the aircraft in the fleet are flown on behalf of Alitalia in Italy.

Eastern Airways operates scheduled flights throughout the UK, particularly on links to Aberdeen and the Shetland Islands of Scotland. They operate examples of the Saab 2000 in their own colours and they also operate some examples in British Airways colours, which usually fly out of London City Airport.

Loganair operates a fleet of Saab 2000s on UK domestic services from Glasgow and Edinburgh.

Skywork Airlines of Switzerland operate two examples on routes from Bern and Basel to European cities.

Tus Airways is a small startup airline based at Larnaca in Cyprus. It flies to Israel and the Greek islands with two leased Saabs.

USA & Canada

PenAir (Peninsula Airways) of Alaska uses three Saab 2000s on scheduled services. The airline has bases in Anchorage, Boston, Denver and Portland, Oregon, so it is feasible for the aircraft to operate anywhere.

Tupolev Tu-134

© Dmitry Belov

A popular and successful Russian aircraft which stood the test of time. The Tu-134 was developed in the 1960s as the country's answer to the Caravelle and DC-9. It was built in the hundreds, but a poor safety record and a shift from older, noisier types have left few in service today, especially since the Russian government passed a requirement for most to be removed from service.

Asia & Middle East

Alrosa still operates a sole example from Mirny to Krasnoyarsk, Irkutsk, Novosirbirsk and Yakustk.

Kazakhstan's **SCAT** is still flying one example out of Almaty.

Air Koryo in North Korea offers flights to those visiting as part of an organised aviation tour. Its aircraft is immaculate, and one of the last Tu-134s built.

Tupolev Tu-154

Arguably the Soviet Union's most successful airliner, the Tu-154 enjoyed many years of success as a workhorse for a lot of airlines. Over 1,000 were produced across the B and M variants, working medium-haul routes across Russia, the CIS and Asia.

Initially popular also in Eastern Europe, all airlines in this region have now removed them from service (Belavia was the last airline to fly the type on schedules).

Asia & Middle East

Air Koryo of North Korea uses its classic Tu-154B-2 and -154M aircraft as part of organised aviation tours to the country.

Alrosa is the only other operator of the TU-154M, and the last commercial airline in Russia to operate the type. The airline is based in Mirny, flying to destinations within Russia both on a charter and scheduled basis. With newer Boeing 737-800s joining the fleet it is only a matter of time before the Tu-154s are retired. Enthusiast tours often organise flights with Alrosa.

Tupolev Tu-204/214

Many took the Tupolev 204 to be Russia's attempt at matching the Boeing 757's place in the market, and it closely resembles the American type. It emerged in 1989 as a possible Tupolev Tu-154 replacement for Soviet airlines, but in retrospect only managed 82 sales.

In 1996 the Tu-204-200, commonly known as the Tu-214, first flew. It offered a higher gross weight and other improvements.

Today a Tu-204SM variant was offered from 2010, with many improvements to the aircraft. Orders which it received have, however, failed to make it to completion and as such the project is on hold.

Africa
Cairo Aviation has three passenger and two cargo Tu-204-120s in its fleet. These mainly operate to destinations around the Mediterranean and Middle East, as well as on domestic services and on behalf of Egypt Air.

Asia & Middle East
Air Koryo of North Korea operates both the Tu-204-100 and 300, which can be flown on if you are on a dedicated aviation tour of North Korea, or flying the airline between Beijing and Pyongyang.

Caribbean
Cubana flies two Tu-204s – one in passenger and one in cargo configurations. Routes vary.

Europe
Red Wings operates a fleet of Tupolev Tu-204s on flights from Moscow to various Russian, Turkish, Red Sea and Mediterranean destinations.

Xian MA60

China's turboprop airliner which closely resembles the Antonov An-24, yet was first flown only in February 2000. It is a stretched variant of the Xian Y-7 from the 1970s.

Not a particularly rare aircraft, with production ongoing. Yet it is very much an indigenous airliner to the Asian region, and has never found its way into some of the more mainline carriers. Therefore enthusiasts consider flying one a rarity.

Asia & Middle East

Cambodia Bayon Airlines is a subsidiary of Joy Air (see below) and operates a small fleet of MA60s between Phnom Penh and Siem Reap.

Joy Air is the largest operator of the type, with over 20 in service and a total order for 66 examples. Based at Xi'an Xianyang Airport in central China.

Nepal Airlines uses two MA60s on domestic flights from its Kathmandu base.

Yakovlev Yak-40

Dating back to the early days of jet airliners, the Yak-40 seemed ahead of its time, being marketed as a commuter aircraft and using three rear-mounted engines. Over 1,000 were built, but precious few remain in service today.

Europe

Artel Staratelei Airlnes, a charter carrier based in Khabarovsk, Russia, is a reclusive airline. Nevertheless it flies three examples.

Motor Sich Airlines operates an example on scheduled services within Ukraine and to Minsk.

Vologda Aviation Enterprise is believed to still use a number of Yak-40s on scheduled domestic routes from its Vologda hub.

Yakovlev Yak-42

© Gennady Misko

The larger brother of the Yak-40, the Yakovlev Yak-42 and -42D were produced between 1979 and 2003. Another three-engined, rear-mounted airliner intended for domestic service within Soviet countries, it enjoyed moderate success.

Europe

Izhavia flies a number of Yak-42s from Izhevsk Airport to Moscow and St. Petersburg.

KrasAvia is a large regional airline based at Krasnoyarsk in eastern Russia. It has a few Yak-42s used on domestic services.

Saratov Airlines is slowly reducing its active fleet of Yak-42s in favour of modern Embraer 195s. You can find them flying to destinations throughout Russia, particularly within Siberia.

Gone But Not Forgotten

These are the classic airliners and aircraft which are now sadly resigned to the history book, at least in terms of flying passengers:

Aerospatiale/BAC Concorde

The joint British and French supersonic airliner graced the skies over the Atlantic for many years. Plenty of people were sad to see it go when both airlines chose to retire the type in 2003.

Airspeed AS.57 Ambassador

Many will have fond memories of this piston airliner from the early days of package tours out of Britain. Only 23 were built and flew passenger services until around 1968.

Avro York

A sturdy aircraft developed from wartime bombers, the York provided much-needed capacity as airlines grew in the 1940s and 50s. The last examples flew with Dan-Air London and Skyways until 1964.

BAC One-Eleven

Although some VIP interior aircraft remain in airworthy condition, the last examples in regular passenger service were retired in Africa around 2008-2009. European Aviation was the last UK operator of the type, retiring it in 2002.

Boeing 247

The luxurious, classic airliner which marked significant progress in design and comfort. 75 were built and flew passenger services between 1933 and World War II.

Boeing 307 Stratoliner

The world's first pressurised airliner, developed from wartime bomber designs. It flew with the legacy carriers in the USA. The last know example in commercial service was retired in 1974.

Boeing 707

Soldiered on until 2014 in the service of Iranian airline Saha Air. Some government and private operators fly the Boeing 707, but not in passenger service.

Boeing 737-100

This, the original model of one of the most successful airliners of all time, was only built in small numbers. The last passenger-carrying examples flew with AeroContinente in Peru, around 2000, and America West Airlines in the USA in 1999.

Boeing 720

The baby of the Boeing 707 family was almost immediately replaced when the Boeing 727 came along. Nevertheless, it soldiered on in passenger service until 1995 when Middle East Airlines retired it. VIP and testbed examples flew on until 2010.

Boeing 727-100

LAB Bolivian Airlines was one of the last carriers to regularly schedule the shorter 727-100 as recently as 2008. This list will soon be joined by the 727-200 as only one airline still flies passengers with it.

Boeing 747-100/200

The original model of the "Jumbo Jet" carried on in passenger service until January 2014 when the final operator, Iran Air, retired its last example EP-IAM. Iran Air was also the last operator of the -200 variant. A failed attempt to start transatlantic 747-200 services by Baltia Airlines recently came to nothing.

Boeing 747SP

Iran Air has continued to resurrect its 747SP 'special performance' aircraft on numerous occasions over recent years. There may even be a chance to fly it again in the future. However, new aircraft deliveries will surely now keep it grounded.

Bristol Britannia

One of the most respected and capable turobprop airliners ever produced, the Britannia sadly came too late as jet airliners were beginning to enter service and airlines looked to this new technology instead of what was seen as more dated. Cubana were the last airline to operate the type in passenger configuration, retiring it in 1990.

Convair 880

Never achieving its goal of competing with the Boeing 707 and Douglas DC-8, only 65 were built. The last passenger service of the Convair 880 was in 1974.

Convair 990

The lengthier version of the 880, the Convair 990 enjoyed even less success with only 37 examples being built. The last passenger flight took place in 1987.

de Havilland Comet

Although it can be argued the Comet flew until 2011 in the form of the RAF's Nimrod aircraft, the original variants – designated the 1, 2 and 4 (only one example of a Comet 3 was built) were retired much earlier. Dan-Air London became famous for buying up as many Comet 4's as they could during the 1970s to supplement their growing charter services. Thus, the airline was the last to fly a passenger-carrying Comet flight in November 1980.

Douglas DC-6

Springbok Classic Air operated a Douglas DC-6 until fairly recently. Any remaining airworthy examples are likely to be found in Alaska flying supplies.

Douglas DC-7

Legendary Airlines restored and operated the last passenger-carrying DC-7B N836D in Fly Eastern Air Lines colours until 2013 when its airworthiness certificate expired. Whether it will ever return to flying remains to be seen.

Douglas DC-8

Airline passenger service on the DC-8 ended in the mid-1990s with MGM Grand Air and Air Marshall Islands, although cargo carrier ATI did operate combi aircraft until recently. All are now retired.

Fokker F27

Whilst it's still feasible that there are F27s flying occasional passenger services in Africa or Argentina, it is thought that no aircraft remain in regular passenger operation. Even cargo examples are few and far between.

Fokker F28

Again, it is thought that at least one F28 is still active in Kenya flying occasional passenger services on domestic or regional routes, it is not thought to be easy to plan or book this. Other airworthy examples remain in government operation.

Hawker Siddeley HS.121 Trident

The last Tridents to fly were retired in the early 1990s when Air China and CAAC sent their examples to training schools and museums. The last flights in the UK occurred on 31st December 1985.

Hawker Siddeley/BAe/Avro 748

After many years of service in the Canadian wilderness, Air North retired its final passenger-carrying examples of this aircraft in 2017. No other operators remain.

Ilyushin IL-14

This workhorse of Soviet and Eastern European skies was affectionately known as the 'Crate'. It worked for passenger, military and cargo operators from its introduction in 1954. Some examples remain airworthy, but none have carried passengers regularly since the early 1980s.

Ilyushin IL-86

Donavia, later Aeroflot-Don, was the last operator of the IL-86 in passenger service. A few Russian Air Force examples are thought to be active.

Lockheed L-188 Electra

This large, modern turboprop was built from 1957 and operated around the world. The last types in regular passenger service were with VARIG in Brazil, and retired in 1992. Reeve Aleutian also operated some examples until 2001 with passenger interiors. Cargo examples remain in operation.

Lockheed L-1011 TriStar

Several examples remained in sporadic use with smaller charter operators in the developing world, alongside the Royal Air Force's tanker and troop transport fleet, which was retired in 2014. Talks of resurrecting this fleet have so far come to nothing.

McDonnell Douglas DC-10

The infamous three-holer remained in service until February 2014, when final carrier Biman Bangladesh retired it. A series of enthusiast flights were held to mark the occasion.

McDonnell Douglas MD-11

KLM was the last operator of the MD-11 in passenger service. It was retired in November 2014 with a number of enthusiast flights from Amsterdam Schiphol. Various examples still fly as freighters around the world.

NAMC YS-11

The Japanese passenger turboprop remained popular in the

Philippines with some smaller carriers into the 2000s, but all have now been retired.

Short 330/360

It's still possible to see some of these 'Sheds' flying cargo around the world, and the smaller SC.7 Skyvan has been in use as a parachute dropping platform. No commercial passenger examples remain in service, however.

Sud Aviacion SE.210 Caravelle

The last scheduled flights of the Caravelle were operated by Gabon Express until the airline went bankrupt in June 2004.

Tupolev Tu-104

One of the classic Soviet designs, and one of the earliest jet airliners to enter service. The type only flew with Aeroflot, and was retired from passenger service in 1979.

Tupolev Tu-114

Once the largest and fastest passenger airliner in service, the Tu-114 was distinguished by its twin sets of propeller blades on each engine. The type was superseded by the Ilyushin IL-62 in 1976, and thus its life was cut short despite an enviable safety and performance record.

Tupolev Tu-144

The Soviet Union's answer to the Concorde and supersonic travel emerged in the shape of the Tu-144, or 'Concordski', as it became known. It lacked commercial appeal and only 55 flights were operated with passengers on board, retiring in 1979. Some occasional flights were operated into the 1980s, but purely for government charter or positioning flights.

Vickers VC-10

The Vickers VC-10's limited career with passenger airlines ended with British Airways in 1981. After this, many of the remaining examples went to the Royal Air Force as tanker and troop transport aircraft. All were retired in September 2013.

Vickers Vanguard

Invicta Air Transport are believed to be the last airline to use the Vanguard in passenger service during the late 1970s. After this, the type enjoyed a renaissance as the 'Merchantmant' cargo carrier, but now all examples are grounded.

Vickers Viscount

The last Viscounts to fly in the UK were retired in 1997 by British World Airlines. Passenger-carrying examples remained in service in Africa for a further few years.

Credits

Paul Mitchell

Airliners Experiences Facebook Page

Airliners.Net

Kevin Stokes

Steve Martin

Sean Burris

President of Classic Jet Tours

Stephen Kinder

Propliner Magazine

Aerodata Quantium Database

FR24.com

Andrew Stewart

Steve Smith on the Yahoo Aeroprints Group

David Wells

Mark Allday

Sam Chui

Charles Kennedy

Olivier Arnaud

Aviation News by Key Publishing

Planespotters.net

Vin Man

David Tweedle

Classic Wings Website

Paul Miller

Francesco Porta

Andrew Lidinson

Ian Faequharson

Francesco Porta

Andrew Martin

Charles Cunliffe

www.tarom.ro

Wikipedia

Jeroen Noordhout

Michael Nelson

Ian Madigan

Roy Blewett's Survivors

Adam Michael

Thomas Murphy

Michael Prophet

Stewart Toone

Bernie Leighton and Boris Vlassov

Other Aviation Books

Preserved Airliners of North America

ISBN 978-0995530799
£9.99

The clear, concise, up-to-date guide on where to find over 600 preserved airframes in Canada, Mexico and the United States. Includes airliners, bizjets and military transport aircraft at museums, airports and in private use.

Lost Airline Colours of Europe

ISBN 978-0993095047
£9.99

Relive the glory days of airliners and liveries from the past in this photographic book. Covers airlines no longer with us, and present-day airlines when they wore very different schemes. Packed full of classic aircraft pictures.